the catcher

the catcher

A Journey in Psychotherapy

Jaime Metcher

the catcher
Copyright © 2021 by Jaime Metcher

Metcher, J
ISBN 978-0-6453253-0-0

All rights reserved. No part of this book may be reproduced in any manner except in the case of brief quotations embedded in critical articles and reviews.

the catcher

"Anyway, I keep picturing all these little kids playing some game in this big field of rye and all. Thousands of little kids, and nobody's around--nobody big, I mean--except me. And I'm standing on the edge of some crazy cliff. What I have to do, I have to catch everybody if they start to go over the cliff - I mean if they're running and they don't look where they're going I have to come out from somewhere and catch them. That's all I do all day. I'd just be the catcher in the rye and all. I know it's crazy, but that's the only thing I'd really like to be. I know it's crazy."

J.D. Salinger

These pages are for and about the person who caught me.

To my catcher

I'm sitting alone on the headland at the point. Just over there is the cliff I could use if I wanted to jump. Not tonight. Probably not ever. My lover says that would be a good place to jump. I think one day she will. If not here then somewhere else. I wonder if I'll know. That will be the fulfilment and completion of my failure, absolute confirmation of the futility of every thing I do and think and feel. And as such, I suppose it doesn't matter if I know or not.

It's a beautiful night. Not a soul in the world knows that I'm here. On the way up I thought, this is a gift too. This silence, this space. Yes, even this solitude. I hate it so much. But I probably need it. Maybe one day I'll look back and appreciate this time.

I could stay here all night. No children, no wife, no lover, no employer – nobody is going to wonder where I am. I've paid in my heart's blood for this freedom, and I am trying to escape it as fast as I can. But in the meantime, costly as it has been, I should appreciate it.

Only you are here. I wonder if you think of me. I think you know I am here. Maybe not this place, but you know I am somewhere like this. When you think of it.

So I am here alone with only my ghosts, you being the most substantial right now. And my lover, who owns every second rib and half a decilitre of each breath. She's always here. And words, again I turn to words.

I've written 150,000 words to my lover, counting the ones I could find. Every syllable useless. Not one scrap of salvation in any of them for her or for me. I bled out the best of me into them. Not nearly enough. Not even close.

I wrote this for her one night, when I was sick of the sound of my voice and all my useless analyses and syntheses and rationalisations:

> Dry words, dead words,
> Litter my bed,
> Bruise my ribs
> While elsewhere
> The warmth of the blood beneath your skin
> The curl of the hair on your neck.
> I toss and turn
> Pieces of broken dreams pierce my skin
> And leave my sheets bloody
> While you breathe and sigh
> In pleasure and in pain
> In another bed.
> Too many words

the catcher

> Clogging my throat
> Sterile and dead
> All of them futile
> Because life is elsewhere.

And now you, more words for you. More words that again will sink to the bottom of the pond. Because you and I already have our parting in view. As is right, and good, and it will be a great day for many reasons. In the meantime, I'm so glad you are here. You are giving birth to my future, and like every childhood we'll know it was good by the way we can leave it behind.

These words, this love, this pouring out of myself. It's something I need to do, and I don't regret any of it. But I so yearn to be giving these gifts to somebody who wants to keep them. Who wants to build something on them.

The yachts are passing by just offshore in the darkness. There's a gentle breeze, cicadas, the sound of the waves at the foot of the cliff.

I was going to come up here and call my family. They are worried about me. Sometimes when I'm too distraught to filter it out I let slip how dark my thoughts are. It terrifies them, and they have no idea what to do or say. Or how to wait out this time with me. Every conversation has to have a conclusion. So in the end, I have to reassure them.

Tonight, when I got here, I didn't want to be reassuring, didn't want to be smoothing over the ugly crevasses in my life for those who can't bear to stare into them with me. So I'm writing to you instead.

I know if you were here, you would be able to be quiet with me, and hear what I'm hearing. The waves, and the cicadas. And my wounds and sorrows wouldn't frighten you. We could look into those pits together. Or not. Just watch the yachts, and laugh at nothing, and at life.

Nov 2016

the catcher

Success

I started therapy out of desperation.

I was being ambushed by sorrow that felled me like a cow in an abattoir. Brought me stunned to my knees where ever I was: at home in the kitchen, at work, walking down the street.

All I wanted from therapy was: make it stop.

And: give me my old life back.

It hasn't stopped, and my old life is gone, gone.

Sorrow is no longer a hammer blow between the eyes. It's a tidal wave, an ocean. It drowns me, spits me up coughing and dazed on the shore of my weekly session.

Every week I crawl into that room utterly without words, beaten speechless by the storms that rage across my ocean, all my words shouted into the wind and snatched away without reaching even my own ears. And every week I fall into the tidepool of my therapist's commitment, sink to the still bottom, and talk without cease, words from a stranger, pages from a story I've never heard.

The story talks about the fabulous creatures that live in the deep, some grotesque, some beautiful. It talks about sunlit days in the shallow lagoons. Building sandcastles on the shore. Swimming naked alone, or with a beautiful friend. The majesty and eternity of the big surf breaking against the cliffs. The beauty and terror of the tempest. And the cold and the dark that's waiting right at the bottom.

I'm learning to live in my ocean. I'm learning to float. And then to swim, and then to fish. One day I'll build a boat, and visit some of the other islands. One day soon.

So...

I wake up crying every morning, and my days are tinted with a watercolour wash of longing. I write and I dream, I'm selfish with friends and generous with strangers. I have a note in my pocket giving me permission to laugh. I am stunned by the beauty of the skies as often as I am by sorrow. I don't want my old life back anymore. Nothing has stopped, but many things have started.

Success.

Dec 2016

Pain

I lead you to my pain. We look at it together. I ask you to get rid of it. You have another idea. You listen to my fears, and wait for me to gather my courage. And then we step into it.

You stay with me when I think I can't bear it anymore. I'm always wrong about that, and you know it. Sometimes we pause, and then wade on.

You say you can see the other side. Blinded by tears, I can only see the next step. But I trust you, so we wade on.

You say that what you can see is a wonderful place. I sob with longing. Just the idea of that place seems like an impossible dream. But you tell me it's real, so we wade on.

There's no other way there. No bridge, no boat. Just the narrow rocky shore we came from, and then this river of pain.

It's getting deeper, harder to wade, harder to keep my head above water. Surely things are getting worse, my life is heading in the wrong direction. No, you say. We are heading in the right direction. There's the other side, where a better life is waiting.

the catcher

I still can't see it. But I still trust you. And you say: if this was easy, you'd already be there. If this didn't hurt, you would have stepped into the river a long time ago. This is hard, and it hurts. But it's the only way to the other side.

I'm afraid that the current will still carry me away before we get there. You say: it might, but you are strong, what you are doing is amazing, what you still can do is wonderful; I believe in you.

I can't feel the bottom anymore, and we are swimming now, buoyed by your belief.

Jan 2017

Becoming 2

Am I asking you to save me
to deny my own agency?
So I can say I didn't want it
but you made me do it?
Life, that is.
Well, whatever –
every life is a collaboration.
Why not partner in this?
Thanks, partner,
I owe you one.
Life, that is.

Jan 2017

the catcher

Becoming 4
Can we touch?
Should we?
Would you run
if I touched you?

Feb 2017

Welcome

I would stumble into your room, shell-shocked. Sit and try to breathe. Let your calm regard draw me out of my pressure suit. And vomit a bucket-load of pain at your feet.

In an hour I would go from wound tight and immobile, to open, to distraught, and to calm again.

And that was what we did. I did tears, and you did soothing. And you played goalie, and blocked my more savage attacks on my self.

But after the opening and in between the tears and while blocking shots, you planted seeds, with names like Acceptance, and Hope. And you carved a little sign and planted it on your consulting room floor, saying "You are welcome here".

And then another, a little bit smaller, saying. "Yes, you. I do mean you.".

the catcher

One day as I was leaving you said: "You know you are welcome here, don't you? The real you?".

"Yes".

"So I don't need these signs anymore, do I?"

"No"

"I know someone who does."

You gave those signs to me, and told me to plant them in my heart, so I would know I was welcome there too.

Feb 2017

Adolescence

When I met you, I was huddled on the couch, and you would spend an hour persuading me to put my feet on the floor. Or just to unfurl enough to take a breath.

Later, we opened rooms, forbidden ordinary rooms, terrifying harmless rooms. An hour was enough, for those domestic journeys. After an hour I needed to rest.

One day you took me into the attic, and we looked out of the dusty windows together, and I saw the horizon for the first time in many years. And I wanted it.

Now I return to you after voyages of discovery, show you my shells and the tentacle marks on my arm from the giant squid. Show you on the map where I fell down the well and couldn't get out for many days, until I remembered how you taught me to climb the ladder to the attic.

I think there are people out there. I've seen the smoke from their camp fires. I've heard them singing at night.

An hour isn't anywhere near enough. Not for the discoveries and the triumphs, not for the dark places I ran from, the fears that turned me away from approaching the camp fires. So now I have to choose. No longer the simplicity of just the couch, and the floor, and my feet.

I know now that hour isn't supposed to be enough. I shouldn't fit into it, and I shouldn't wish for it to expand. I am supposed to outgrow it, and take my stories and my scars and my fears and the view to that horizon out in to a much larger space.

This is adolescence. I'm not ready to leave. But I'm ready to start wanting to.

Feb 2017

Catch me

I realised
that all I wanted to say is:
I'm so sad
and I just need to tell someone
and you're the only person
I can tell
who will have any idea
of why

March 2017

the catcher

Catechism

Yesterday a man died. One of many.

He was swept off the rocks and died in the ocean. I wished I was him. Dying in the ocean would be like going home. The only part I didn't like is that they found his body and tried to revive him. Interrupted his peaceful sinking and the nibbling of the fish. You can't blame them. But it seems disrespectful.

He didn't want to die. Well, there is no justice in the world, is there? If it could be arranged that death came for me, and I could spare you the pain of my choosing; well, that could work. Not exactly win-win, but it could work. Tell the angels: spare someone else; take me.

But wait: someone is slamming their fist on the table. "HOLD THAT TELEGRAM!!".

You, my beautiful catcher, reminding me of your ferocity.

"Live. First because I want you to. Then because you want to. In that order."

Psychic mirror neurons: you are there each week, so I am there each week; you don't give up, so I don't give up. My heartbeat slows to match yours, and the steady rhythm of your breathing becomes mine. And then your anger reminds me that I have fire in me too. Not only rain.

"Is there beauty in the world?
Is there love in your heart?"

Yes. And yes. And so?

"What other reason do you need?"

March 2017

The win

Oh
fuck
I want you to win.
Oh God I want that
for you.
You deserve the win.
I want to give that to you
then I can leave.

March 2017

the catcher

Outside

I am in a chair. I am in a cot. I'm trying to sit up straight. I'm lying on my back, reaching up. You are in front of me on the computer screen. You are leaning over me, about to pick me up and hold me. I'm trying to breathe. I can hardly see through the tears.

All there is in the world is your face, your beautiful smile, and your soothing voice.

I met you at my front gate, all those months ago, and invited you in. We sat on the porch of the gatehouse and chatted. Difficult stuff, to be sure. On the porch of the gatehouse, serious topics can be discussed.

Over the months that followed I invited you in again and again, further into my world, until we were in my private room in the heart of the citadel.

In that room serious topics can be discussed, and shame, and humiliation, and vulnerability. Things I'd never talked about with anybody. We made many discoveries there, and wrote them on the walls. But always we were in my room, in the citadel of my mind, writing thoughts on the walls.

And then we discovered, you showed me, you let me discover, an inescapable truth. My mind was going to kill me, almost certainly, and there was nowhere left to hide. No deeper sanctuary, no more secure walls, no more elaborate defenses. The enemy was within and always would be. In here is the courtroom where I sentenced myself to death for the transgressions of loss and failure and grief, and in here is the scaffold.

We retraced our steps, out through the keeps and curtain walls, libraries and beautiful gardens, to that monstrously strong gate.

Only in my last and deepest refuge could you have convinced me to come out and step through that gate, and back into my body.

So I'm in a chair, not lying on my couch, sitting up straight, not curled around my pain, breathing deeply, not sipping at air through a clenched throat. I'm so far outside what I have come to know as myself that I can only understand it by going back to a time before the first stone of the fortress was laid.

While my mind is screaming "Disaster!" and promising safety and offering doom, you and I are reciting together this poem and enchantment and unspeakable heresy:

Your mind is wrong. Trust your body.
Your mind is wrong. Trust your body.
Your mind is wrong. Trust your body.

the catcher

My mind wants to die. My body is hungry and wants to eat and drink. My mind thinks my life is shit. My body knows that this bed is warm, and the skin of my lover feels good against mine. My mind can't believe anyone could love me. My body smiles back when you smile at me.

Start again. The gates can be open, I can come and go, the citadel doesn't have to be a trap. I can stop work on that scaffold, and maybe one day use the wood for something more worthwhile.

May 2017

Hello sky

The catcher asked me why I'm alive. "Why are you still here?" Her beautiful gentle voice.

I smiled through tears. What a lovely question. Not what's wrong with you; why do you want to die; how can we keep you back from the edge; but, why are you still here.

Every now and then the catcher reaches effortlessly through layers of defenses and anguish, through shattered and razor sharp shards of armour, through the cracked and weeping skin of my blasted epidermis and puts her hand gently on my heart.

The storms still and the demon hosts pause for minute, lean on their swords and chat gutturally but quietly amongst themselves while I consider her question.

In the stillness of the pause I hear her voice in my head telling me this: you are alive. You have chosen; thus far you have chosen. Whatever courage it requires, you have it. Whatever capacity for pain, you have it. You have been tested, and up to this point you have not been found wanting. So – why did you choose as you did?

Why are you alive?

My little army of apologists and defense attorneys, most of whom are on the take, or moles for the prosecution, leapt to their feet harrumphing and marshalling eloquent phrases about living for others, sparing my family the pain and bewilderment of my premature departure. But before they could speak, a child's voice rang out, clear and strong.

Hello, I thought. I haven't heard you this clearly since – oh, were we five years old? Walking barefoot on the beach in winter, looking in all the rockpools, perfectly comfortable wrapped in the ragged grey cloak of the sky and with periwinkles scattered across my brow. Hello me. Where have you been all this time?

We, me and him, we said, I said: because the world is so beautiful.

The sky doesn't care about my shame. The sunrise doesn't know about my failures. The waves roll over my head the same whether it's full of pain or only thoughts of kelp. This city behind its tideline breathes and bustles and turns in its sleep regardless of whether I'm awake counting my sorrows or dreaming of lovers past and future.

the catcher

Because the world is so beautiful, I said, looking out the window at the sky. Hello sky. Hello me.

May 2017

Heartbeat

It's a magical incantation
a vital rhythm
the slowest heartbeat in the world
but the most reliable
one hour
each pulse lasts
once a week
and in that rushing
of life's blood
we soar.
The iron law
forbids three things
that forbidding like
a pentagram drawn
in salt creates
the space for
everything.

June 2017

Lullaby

The tigers came again while I was sleeping and ripped my belly open. The wine didn't keep them away. I can't tell anyone about them, and they know, and are laughing. I woke up and hung out my washing while holding my guts in with one hand, wondering if it's a good thing that at least I'll have clean underwear for when I can take a breath again. Or if I'm just folding my jacket neatly before stepping in front of the train.

I want to be held, and you are right, your comfort is a poor, weak thing. I'm right too, there's a universe in your eyes. But I want to be held.

I can't tell anyone and you are all I have. Sing me to sleep, dear catcher. Sing me to sleep.

Sep 2017

Someday

When
my catcher says
"someday
someone will love you"
I weep the
thick, heavy tears
of absolute loss
while searching for
the courage
to hope.

Oct 2017

the catcher

Lessons

I learned that even the worst times will end. That after a day of struggling to breathe, there could still be a moment of stillness, and the beauty of a sunset could be the only thought in my head. I learned to expect it, and wait for it, and rely on it. When I was curled up on the floor unable to do anything, still there was room for a little voice saying "I know how this goes. I'll wait it out. I don't know how long it will take, but I can wait it out."

I learned to stop fighting the pain and accept it. I came to see it sometimes as a teacher, sometimes just as bad weather. I learned to ride it, and sometimes when it overwhelmed me like a wave, just go loose and wait for it to stop pounding me into the sand.

I learned how hard it is to trust, and that it is possible.

I learned that I'm not always wrong, that I didn't always misunderstand, and that some of my pain is from attempting to fold myself into realities that other people have twisted for their own reasons. Sometimes, when I hurt, it's possible that I've been wronged. Not that I'm wrong. Not always.

the catcher

I learned not to be alone, not to try to be alone and self-sufficient and totally independent. Disconnectedness is madness. But I learned also that the price of connection shouldn't be all of my self-respect and self-worth.

I learned that being abandoned is a habit I learned a long time ago. Feeling alone in the world is a lesson that I learned. It's not a flaw I was born with.

I learned that my barriers are either total, or non-existent. Once lowered I neither ask or expect reciprocity, respect, consideration, kindness, understanding. Once lowered I can never raise them again. Once someone is inside, there is no unreasonable behaviour.

I did not learn to get over it, or move on, or let go, or man up. I did not learn to stop caring or stop feeling. The grief didn't stop, and the pain didn't stop.

I learned that I'm ashamed of who and what I am, in every aspect and at all times. I learned that my idea of my place in the world is no place, that ideally I should be invisible and take up no space. From the few moments of the few days that I've been able to live with my head up and my eyes on the horizon, I've realized that I live under a crushing weight without knowing it.

I don't have permission to be here. I need permission, and I don't have it. So I live in a tiny illicitly-carved out space, and try to avoid being noticed.

Pain and grief and betrayal and confusion make life wearisome, but they don't kill me. Shame might. I don't want to live with pain, but it's the shame of being someone who lives with pain and can't get over it that's really unbearable. The shame of being someone who is devastated by loss. It will make people uncomfortable. It will make people feel bad. It will attract pity, or contempt, or even just irritation. It will be noticed. I should stop being that person, or just stop being.

I haven't learned to even get hold of the shame, it slips away from me. But I have learned to see it.

Dec 2017

the catcher

Know that you are allowed the comfort of arms that you might not be able to hold on to forever- we all are.

- my anonymous catcher

Jan 2018

Company

You bring me to the door
again and again
hold my trembling hand
pour your voice over my aching soul.
You hold me although
the jagged pieces of me
cut your skin.
I refuse to open my eyes
so you tell me what you can see.
And when I turn away without stepping through
and climb back down into my hell
you climb down with me
to keep me company.

April 2018

Enough

Adolescence. I've grown up. I've taken a step away, and then another, and I'm not afraid.

I've fallen into your eyes so many times, and now it seems I've fallen through, and no matter how far I go I'm still within. Still enclosed, and still safe.

So I stretch the string, but it doesn't get tighter, nor does it let go. It hurts, yes, like stretching a tired muscle hurts, or a healing wound. It hurts like trying and succeeding hurts, not like trying and failing hurts. I know it hurts you too, and I know you are glad of it, because that's the price and it's a tiny, tiny price compared to the reward.

Now the air has changed and the colour has changed, and it's the colour of your eyes and the colour of your smile. Yours, and those of the kind people and the brave people and the steadfast people, those who were always there and those who have just arrived. The people I didn't notice because I was burning my eyes with the electric glare of the ones I wanted, the ones whose arc would burn away the self I hated, the ones who would play their part in my project of annihilation.

The kind and the brave and the steadfast. I don't have to purchase pleasure at the price of a soul-deep ache. I don't have to pay for being happy.

My deepest joy was in moments of respite from the crushing pain of being myself. I sought the pain and I sought the arduous ascent. I was able to find a fleeting self-worth in the sacrifice and self-denial and endurance it took to reach those summits, those impossible places. But there's no rest on an airless peak. Only an inevitable descent, a battle that leaves me weaker, not stronger, and then nothing but another attempt.

But it's changed. The kind and the brave don't have peace, but they fight their battles, and win, and gain more than they lose, and add to the sum of happiness. Not always, but enough. We add to each other instead of exacting a price. Down here in the green valleys joy can add to joy, and self can add to self. I can add joy. I can join the dance. I am enough.

Oct 2018

the catcher

www.ingramcontent.com/pod-product-compliance
Lightning Source LLC
Chambersburg PA
CBHW070312010526
44107CB00056B/2572